Exploring Planets
JUPITER

Susan Ring

WEIGL PUBLISHERS INC.

Published by Weigl Publishers Inc.
350 5th Avenue, Suite 3304, PMB 6G
New York, NY USA 10118-0069
Web site: www.weigl.com
Copyright 2004 WEIGL PUBLISHERS INC.

Library of Congress Cataloging-in-Publication Data

Ring, Susan.
  Jupiter / by Susan Ring.
     v. cm. -- (Exploring planets)
Includes index.
Contents: Introducing Jupiter -- What's in a name? -- Jupiter spotting
-- Early observations -- Jupiter in the solar system -- Jupiter and
Earth -- Missions to Jupiter -- Jupiter explorer -- Jupiter on the web
-- Activity : Jupiter math -- What have you learned?
  ISBN 1-59036-103-2 (lib. bdg. : alk. paper) – ISBN 1-59036-230-6 (pbk.)
  1. Jupiter (Planet)--Juvenile literature. [1. Jupiter (Planet)] I.
Title. II. Series.
  QB661 .R56 2003
  523.45--dc21
                              2002014562

Printed in the United States of America
1 2 3 4 5 6 7 8 9 0 08 07 06 05 04

Photograph Credits

Every reasonable effort has been made to trace ownership and to obtain permission to reprint copyright material. The publishers would be pleased to have any errors or omissions brought to their attention so that they may be corrected in subsequent printings.

Cover: Photos.com (top); Tom Stack & Associates (bottom)

Virginia Boulay: page 12; **CORBIS/MAGMA:** pages 8 (Roger Ressmeyer), 16 (Bettmann); **Digital Vision:** pages 1, 4, 14L; **Hulton Archive by Getty Images:** pages 6, 10; **NASA:** pages 7, 9, 17, 18, 19; **NASA/Tom Stack & Associates:** pages 13, 14R; **PhotoSpin, Inc.:** page 21; **Tom Stack & Associates:** pages 3, 22.

Project Coordinator Jennifer Nault **Design** Terry Paulhus **Substantive Editor** Heather Kissock
Copy Editor Michelle Lomberg **Layout** Bryan Pezzi **Photo Researcher** Tina Schwartzenberger

Contents

Introducing Jupiter 4

Name That Planet 6

Jupiter Spotting 8

Early Observations 10

Jupiter in Our Solar System 12

Jupiter and Earth 14

Missions to Jupiter 16

Planet People 18

Jupiter on the Internet 20

Young Scientists at Work 21

What Have You Learned? 22

Words to Know/Index 24

Introducing Jupiter

Jupiter is the largest planet in our **solar system**. It is twice the size of all the other planets combined. For hundreds of years, scientists have been curious about Jupiter. They have discovered that the planet has swirling gases, forceful winds, and a powerful **magnetic field**. Read on to find out more about this gigantic planet.

■ Jupiter looks like it has stripes. These "stripes" are actually layers of cloud.

Jupiter Facts

- It takes 12 years for Jupiter to revolve around the Sun. Earth revolves around the Sun in 365 days.

- Jupiter has the largest storm ever seen on any planet. The storm is a hurricane twice the size of Earth.

- Like Saturn, Jupiter has rings around it. Jupiter's three rings are very dark and cannot be seen with ordinary telescopes.

- The clouds around Jupiter move at speeds of about 400 miles per hour (644 kilometers per hour).

- There is more than twice as much **gravity** on Jupiter as there is on Earth.

Name That Planet

In Roman **mythology**, Jupiter is the leader of all other gods. He is the god of light and sky, and protects the state and its laws.

The ancient Romans built a temple to Jupiter. This temple was very important to them. It was here that wars were declared and treaties were signed.

In Greek mythology, this same god is called Zeus.

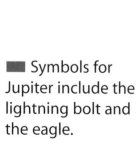 Symbols for Jupiter include the lightning bolt and the eagle.

Jupiter Moons

Astronomers have discovered 39 moons around Jupiter. The four largest moons are Ganymede, Europa, Io, and Callisto. Ganymede is the largest moon in the entire solar system. Europa is covered with a layer of ice that is 60 miles (97 km) thick. Io has active volcanoes. Callisto is believed to have an ocean below its surface.

■ Io, Europa, Ganymede, and Callisto are called the Galilean satellites. Together, these satellites are named for their discoverer.

Jupiter Spotting

Sometimes during its **orbit**, Earth comes between Jupiter and the Sun. When this happens, we can see Jupiter in the night sky. Viewed through a telescope, the planet looks like a small disk. It is cream-colored and shines brightly, like a star. Bands of dark and light clouds can be seen spread across the disk. Jupiter is one of the brightest objects in the night sky.

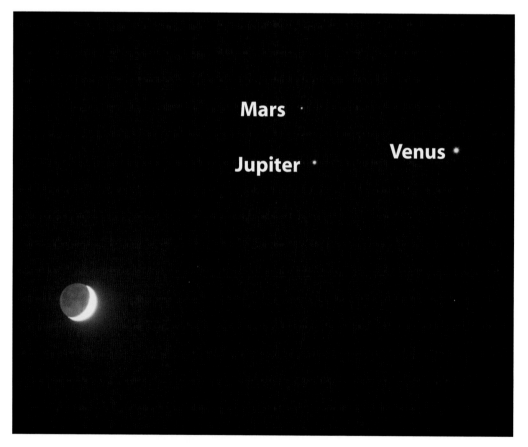

Jupiter is not as bright as Venus, but outshines Mars in the night sky.

See for Yourself

When viewed through binoculars, several of Jupiter's moons can be seen from Earth. Jupiter can sometimes be seen without a telescope. Check with your local **planetarium** or on the Internet to find the best times and places to view Jupiter and its moons.

■ Telescopes that detect heat in space can detect erupting volcanoes on Io.

Early Observations

Jupiter shines so brightly that people have seen it in the night sky since ancient times.

The first astronomer to study Jupiter was an Italian named Galileo Galilei. In 1610, he discovered that Jupiter had moons. The moons moved around the planet in an orbit. This observation proved that the planets did not orbit Earth, as was once believed.

In 1610, Galileo wrote a book about his discoveries.

Galileo Galilei

Galileo Galilei is one of the most important scientists in history. He was the first person to use a telescope to look at the planets. Galileo used a telescope that he created himself. It was much more powerful than any telescope developed before.

Through his telescope, Galileo viewed the Moon. He took notes and described its surface for the first time. Galileo also risked blindness by using the telescope to look at the Sun. The risk proved worthwhile when he discovered sunspots. Sunspots are dark patches that appear on the surface of the Sun. They are very magnetic.

Galileo also directed his telescope toward Jupiter. Through it, he discovered Jupiter's four largest moons.

Jupiter in Our Solar System

Jupiter is one of the nine planets in our solar system. It is the fifth planet from the Sun.

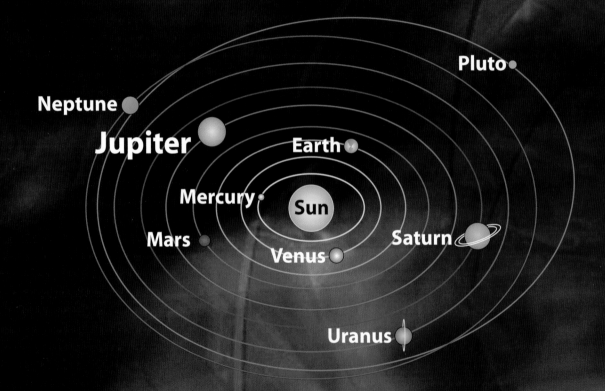

Pluto

Neptune

Jupiter

Earth

Mercury

Sun

Mars

Saturn

Venus

Uranus

Jupiter's surface holds gases that move in bands of orange, red, and yellow.

The Great Red Spot is a large storm that has never stopped. Astronomers have watched it whirl for more than 300 years.

Jupiter and Earth

Jupiter and Earth are two very different planets. Size is the main difference. Jupiter is more than 11 times wider than Earth. In fact, Earth could be placed inside Jupiter's Great Red Spot twice, and there would still be space left over. The larger planet also has 318 times more **mass** than Earth. Even though Jupiter is larger than Earth, it spins faster on its **axis**. A day on Earth is 24 hours. On Jupiter, a day is only about 10 hours.

■ The Sun helps produce weather on Earth. Jupiter is farther away from the Sun. Its weather may be produced by the planet's internal heat.

Compare the Planets

PLANET FEATURES

PLANET	Distance from the Sun	Days to Orbit the Sun	Diameter	Length of Day	Average Temperature
Mercury	36 million miles (58 million km)	88	3,032 miles (4,880 km)	4,223 hours	333° Fahrenheit (167° C)
Venus	67 million miles (108 million km)	225	7,521 miles (12,104 km)	2,802 hours	867° Fahrenheit (464° C)
Earth	93 million miles (150 million km)	365	7,926 miles (12,756 km)	24 hours	59° Fahrenheit (15° C)
Mars	142 million miles (229 million km)	687	4,222 miles (6,975 km)	25 hours	−81° Fahrenheit (−63° C)
Jupiter	484 million miles (779 million km)	4,331	88,846 miles (142,984 km)	10 hours	−230° Fahrenheit (−146° C)
Saturn	891 million miles (1,434 million km)	10,747	74,897 miles (120,535 km)	11 hours	−285° Fahrenheit (−176° C)
Uranus	1,785 million miles (2,873 million km)	30,589	31,763 miles (51,118 km)	17 hours	−355° Fahrenheit (−215° C)
Neptune	2,793 million miles (4,495 million km)	59,800	30,775 miles (49,528 km)	16 hours	−355° Fahrenheit (−215° C)
Pluto	3,647 million miles (5,869 million km)	90,588	1,485 miles (2,390 km)	153 hours	−375° Fahrenheit (−226° C)

Missions to Jupiter

The first **space probe** sent to Jupiter was launched in 1972. It was called *Pioneer 10.* While traveling past Jupiter in 1973, *Pioneer 10* took many pictures and measurements of the planet and its moons. This information was sent back to Earth so that scientists could learn more about Jupiter. Since then, six other probes have journeyed to the giant planet. The probes have taken pictures and have gathered other information using radar.

■ Information gathered by *Pioneer 10* helped scientists design future space probes to Jupiter.

Life on Jupiter?

Very little is known about Jupiter's surface. The average temperature at the top of the clouds is about -230° Fahrenheit (-146° C). Powerful winds swirl at great speeds and blow deadly gases in all directions. People could not survive in these conditions. Recent **data** from the *Galileo* space probe shows that there might be water on Jupiter's moon, Europa. This means that some form of life could be possible.

■ Scientists are designing a space probe to detect if there is water on Europa.

Planet People

Classroom Astronomers

Name: Classroom astronomers

Jupiter Accomplishments: Helped control radio telescopes that gathered data from Jupiter

Students in 13 different states were part of a team exploring Jupiter. They helped control large **radio telescopes** in California. The telescopes gathered data from NASA's space probe *Cassini* as it passed Jupiter. The students' work was done from their classrooms using computers.

This program is called the Goldstone Apple Valley Radio Telescope Project, known as GAVRT.

■ The Goldstone Deep Space Communication Complex is in California's Mojave Desert.

Randy G. Herrera

Name: Randy G. Herrera
Jupiter Accomplishments:
Works on the *Galileo*
space probe

Randy is the Science Coordinator for the Radio Science Team on the space probe *Galileo*. He helps plan and keep track of *Galileo's* radio experiments.

Randy grew up in Texas. As a boy, he liked to take his electric toys apart and put them back together. This curiosity led him to study electrical engineering in college.

Every day is different for Randy and his team. "It's really exciting to think ... that we are exploring space right now," he says.

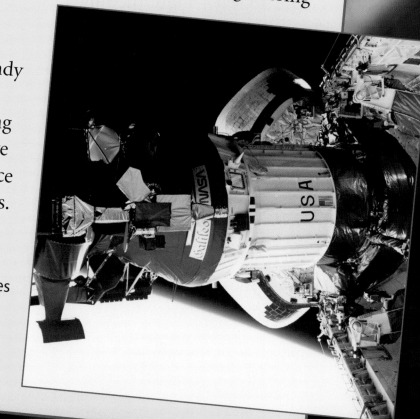

■ The space probe *Galileo* captured images of a comet colliding with Jupiter in 1994.

Jupiter on the Internet

To learn more about Jupiter, look for books at your school library. The Internet is also an excellent place to learn about Jupiter. There are many great Web sites with information. Just type the words *Jupiter* and *planet* into a search engine. Google and Yahoo are useful search engines.

The Internet has information on all of the planets in our solar system. To learn about the nine planets, visit these Web sites:

Encarta Homepage
www.encarta.com
Type the name of a planet that you would like to learn about into the search engine.

NASA Kids
http://kids.msfc.nasa.gov
NASA built a Web site for young learners just like you. Visit this site to learn more about the nine planets, space travel, and the latest NASA news.

Young Scientists at Work

Calculate Your Age on Jupiter

When you celebrate your birthday, you are actually celebrating one trip around the Sun. This is because we celebrate birthdays once every 365 days. If you lived on another planet and celebrated your birthday every time that planet went around the Sun, your age would be different.

How old would you be if you lived on Jupiter? It takes 12 Earth years for Jupiter to make one trip around the Sun. So, to calculate your age on Jupiter, divide your Earth age by 12.

(Your age) $\div$ 12 = _____

What Have You Learned?

How much do you know about Jupiter?
Test your knowledge!

1 Who was Jupiter named for?

2 Of the nine planets, how does Jupiter rank in size?

3 How long is a day on Jupiter?

4 What are the names of Jupiter's four biggest moons?

5 Can Jupiter be seen without a telescope?

6 What is the name of the huge storm on Jupiter?

7 Which astronomer discovered Jupiter's moons?

8 True or False?
It is too cold for people to live on Jupiter.

9 How many Earth years equal 1 year on Jupiter?

10 True or False?
Jupiter has rings around it.

What was your score?

9–10   You should work at NASA!

5–8   Not too bad for an earthling!

0–4   You need to polish your telescope!

Answers

1 Jupiter was named for the Roman leader of all gods. **2** Jupiter is the largest of all the planets. **3** One day on Jupiter lasts 10 hours. **4** Jupiter's four largest moons are Ganymede, Io, Europa, and Callisto. **5** Yes **6** The huge storm is called the Great Red Spot. **7** Galileo Galilei first discovered Jupiter's moons. **8** True. The weather can be colder than -200° Fahrenheit (-129° C). **9** One year on Jupiter equals 12 Earth years. **10** True. Jupiter has three rings.

Words to Know

astronomers: people who study space and its objects

axis: an imaginary line on which a planet spins

data: information collected in order to find specific answers

gravity: the force that pulls objects together

magnetic field: an invisible area where a planet has the power to affect magnetic objects

mass: size or bulk

mythology: stories and legends about heroes and gods

orbit: the nearly circular path a space object makes around another object in space

planetarium: a place where stars and planets can be observed

radio telescopes: devices that pick up radio waves from space

solar system: the Sun, the planets, and other objects that move around the Sun

space probe: a spacecraft used to gather information about space

Index

Earth 5, 8, 9, 10, 12, 14, 15, 16, 21

Galilei, Galileo 10, 11
GAVRT 18
Great Red Spot 13, 14

Herrera, Randy 19

moons 7, 9, 10, 11, 16, 17
mythology 6

Pioneer 10 16

space probes 16, 17, 19
Sun 5, 8, 11, 12, 14, 15, 21

temperature 15, 17